Three Obituaries and an Afternoon Tea

John Watson

Three Obituaries and an Afternoon Tea

Three Obituaries and an Afternoon Tea
ISBN 978 1 76109 129 2
Copyright © text John Watson 2021

First published 2012 by Picaro Press

This edition published 2021 by
GINNINDERRA PRESS
PO Box 3461 Port Adelaide 5015
www.ginninderrapress.com.au

Contents

Jeanne Claude (1935–2009)	7
Poland to Egypt: Sophie Moss (1917–2009)	17
A Mandelbrot Set	27
Homage to Chekhov	45

Jeanne Claude (1935–2009)

1   On first seeing Christo Javacheff
    And falling in love as rapidly
    As the breeze would later stir Little Bay

    She changes the locks on her apartment
    And addresses her husband thus,
    'Your key no longer fits my lock.'

2   Recalling Suzie Quatro's cheerful but unequivocal
    'I hear you knocking but you can't come in,'
    She leaves her husband like a parcel left

    Wrapped and pensive on a shelf,
    And begins with Christo the first day
    Of the rest of her life.

3   This pronouncement, 'Your key et cetera,' announces
    The calm configuration begun years before
    On that same shared June day in 1935

    When she and Christo were born, a day
    As singular as the sun's blue shadow on snow
    Moving as it moves out of cloud.

4   Commissioned to paint a portrait
    Of the wife of General de Guilleborn
    Christo attended their Paris apartment

    And met their daughter Jeanne Claude,
    A conventionally married young woman
    Soon to wrap herself in billowing destiny.

5 Like recollection's pebble falling
   Into the millpond of Consciousness
   She has already fallen in love

   When Christo takes off his glasses
   And takes chamomile tea having completed
   Preliminary sketches of her mother.

6 At the beginning of *Aeneid* 8, Jeanne Claude says,
   Is the most remarkably expressive figure:
   Aeneas' state of uncertainty

   Is likened to the reflection of water
   Shimmering and moving on a wall;
   Just so Jeanne Claude on first seeing Christo.

7 Aeneas in this uncertain state
   Stands unknowingly at the mouth of the Tiber.
   The god of the Tiber appears

   And promises to reverse the currents
   To enable his progress upstream;
   Just so her vast wrapped future.

8 Born in Casablanca on the same day
   As her future partner, Jeanne Claude
   Has already established the refrain:

   'Of all the enswathed trapezoids in all the world,
   Of all the wrapped observation decks,
   That you should walk into mine…

9   Of all the vast plateaux and declivities,
All the clamouring stretches of coastline
Waiting to be covered,

    Of all the armatures of the world
Waiting to regain their original innocence,
Let us spread a tablecloth over these.'

10   Arriving in Sydney in 1969
To wrap the rock platform of Little Bay
In 92,900 square metres of fabric,

    She is photographed at a press conference
Wearing a beret or cap and looking
Like Jeanne Moreau in *Jules and Jim*.

11   Little Bay behind the hospital
Will look briefly like a patient in bandages
Improvised by a generous, genial nurse

    Distracted by conversation and laughter.
The coast will look like a long low lumpy
Newspaper parcel of vegetable peelings.

12   Little Bay, wrapped to look
Disconcertingly and therefore pleasingly
Like something else, recalls perhaps

    The amusing teatowel image
Of the Opera House pictured
As plates stacked on a washing-up rack.

13 Revelation by enswathement
   Is implicit in the appearance
   Of Little Bay years after the event

   As if it were remembering still
   Its ten weeks under wraps
   During which time it dwelt on its past.

14 Dust haze hangs over water acres,
   Proximate escarpments seem obscurely visible,
   Seabirds are wary of leaving shallows;

   Noon hangs heavily, as uncertain
   As a field curlew. 'The absence of presence'
   (Jeanne Claude) cries out to be constrained.

15 The brevity of the dragonfly alighting
   Translates into the project manifesto:
   That something twenty years in the planning

   With consultations, interviews and negotiations
   Will vanish from the world
   After a few dragonfly days.

16 And the dragonfly brevity of the day
   Is a single Fraunhofer line
   Across the spectrum of the centuries,

   Widening in art which voices
   (Jeanne Claude:) 'The quality of love and tenderness
   We humans hold for what does not last.'

17 92,900 square metres of aluminised fabric,
    56 kilometres of polypropylene rope,
    25,000 fasteners and threaded studs

    Deployed opposite the leprosarium ruins
    And the remains of its wall which once
    Segregated men and women.

18 For ten weeks of daily scrutiny
    The sea came from far and wide,
    Dragging the moon in its puzzlement

    And at low tide dragging the chain
    In listless animated attention
    Studied this seventy day artifice.

19 The tarpaulins anchored over the rock platform
    By 15 professional mountain climbers
    And an army of trained volunteers

    Were one day covered by a sea mist.
    Then, as if metaphor had stepped
    Down from the saddle, memory walked abroad.

20 For her baccalaureate in Latin (1952)
    Jeanne Claude had encountered in the *Aeneid*
    The concept of scale enlargement and grandeur

    So that the notion of wrapping a parcel
    Would naturally extend itself
    To valleys, cliffs and foreshores.

21 Valleys, cliffs and foreshores
   Give off an ozone of exuberance
   Which Jeanne Claude embodies

   As she oversees the hauling
   Of 10,000 oil drums and bales of paper
   And tarpaulins, by a team of dragonfly abseilers.

22 A steeplejack lowers himself
   From the crane through the admiring air
   Full of the Marianne Moore poem about him.

   Waterbeetling trapezists and abseilers
   Scale the curtained Pont Neuf calling
   'Jeanne Claude! Your son's a poet!'

23 Lipstick-pink round the eleven islands
   Of Biscaynes Bay, Miami
   Like Al Jolson singing Mamm-y

   Or like saltwater crocs
   Surfacing and submerging off Florida
   In lipstick-pink tutus.

24 'Let us have extended tutorials
   On the perpetually temporary
   Absence of subject;

   Let us make apple-pie beds
   Over the earth's familiar mattress
   To startle the reticent into confidences.'

25 'Let us fly flags, umbrellas, curtains,
   Saffron wind gates that are not gates
   But banners or proscenium curtains

   Billowing open on a performance
   Largely invented by the audience
   As they crowd in to marvel at its curtains.'

26 Absence of subject, art's ultimate ideal,
   Closely relates to absence of purpose
   Or presence of delayed purpose

   In the body: the appendix, the adolescent breast,
   DNA codes pervasively implicit,
   Cells waiting like a suspension in music.

27 Covering the legs of the piano – a joke?
   Christo (1996): 'Now that my hair
   Has turned grey and Jeanne Claude's

   Has turned red' (laughter)… Laughter
   Is implicit in wrapping a cliff
   Or town hall like a birthday surprise.

28 The presence of body organs, pumping and jumping trip
   Wires and secreting secretly and pulsing
   And generally getting on with it

   Beneath cascading visible beauty, might suggest –
   If another were needed – another
   Rationale for the draped object.

29 And the Pont Neuf or Reichstag
   Entirely covered in modest drapes
   Such as were thought in former times suitable

   To cover the legs of pianos
   Might suggest also the mysterious dynamics
   Of force-at-a-distance.

30 Jeanne Claude eats a nectarine
   And looks again at the Pont Neuf,
   Vulnerable, incomplete, hopeful

   Like the raised head of a dog
   Waiting to be taken for a walk,
   And begins applying to local authorities.

31 10,000 communications with authorities,
   Petty clerks, chief petty officers, councillors, burgomasters,
   Panjandrums, magnates, managers and sub-managers,

   Represent ten years of slow dancing and waiting
   During which the body cells of Christo
   And Jeanne Claude are several times renewed.

32 Jeanne Claude standing in the swimming pool
   Writes letters to bureaucrats
   On a pad resting on the boardwalk:

   'I am hoping by wrapping your town hall
   To restore the mystery of distance
   So eloquently recalled by blackbirds singing.'

33　Swallows low-skimming in cusps,
　　Discoursing or at least being discursive,
　　Turn alternately silver and dusk-grey

　　Across the face of the mastaba.
　　Jeanne Christo on her mobile phone laughs,
　　'A mastaba is a truncated rectangular pyramid.'

34　Stormclouds like a sack of coal dust
　　Being shouldered by a mountain; a dusk rainbow;
　　Shimmering rain undeterred by lightning;

　　Then at noon that same rain returning as vapour.
　　None elicits the least glance or remark
　　From the curtains striding through the valley.

35　Jeanne Claude explains over coffee
　　The concept of the wrapped article:
　　'We reveal the uncertainty of memory,

　　The flavour or fragrance of lemon or rhubarb
　　Faintly present in a rich madeira cake,
　　Even the absence of a loved one.'

36　Next were to be thousands of unfurled umbrellas
　　Seen by hundreds of thousands of visitors
　　In the open countryside: in Japan

　　Blue, the blue of cherry blossom skies,
　　And at the same time in California
　　Yellow, the yellow of Californian poppies.

37 The Mastaba, which after her death
   Is still to be realised in the United Emirates,
   Will require 110,000 oil barrels configured

   As a truncated rectangular pyramid,
   A platform for rhetoric or declamation
   Or a full moon draining back molten gold.

38 A platform for the rising moon
   Might recall the huge inflated cylinder
   And its two mammoth cranes

   In Kassel, Germany, in 1968,
   Their elongated parcel of rosewater air
   (Or so it seemed) 80 metres tall.

39 But now Jeanne Claude is elsewhere
   In process of gestation or osmosis
   Through semi-permeable membrane. She is already

   Applying to higher authorities to construct
   'Clouds elevated by seagoing cranes'
   Or 'Picture of an Aeroplane Just Out of Sight.'

40 Jeanne Claude: 'Happiness is our only subject,'
   Happiness like birds singing but hidden,
   Like the cabin in the woods blurred in rain shine.

   Consider then these very woods themselves hidden
   Under canvas and stout boy scout knots;
   Jeanne Claude: 'Mystery is happiness,
             happiness mystery.'

Poland to Egypt: Sophie Moss (1917–2009)

Her Name
Zofia Roza Marie
Jadwiga Elzbieta
Katarzyna Ariela Tarnowski.

Birth
March 16, 1917
'Arrival with glances
Promising mischief.'

Place of Birth
Rudnik, Poland,
A forested estate,
Parents as distracted as trees.

Rudnik
The forest glooming
Dark as shadows
Of Gdansk masts at dusk.

Dusk
A cow bell;
The notion of a meadow
Implicit with moisture.

Moisture
We can't go on
Meeting like this
Say sun and rain.

Further Lyrics
The towering trees,
The towelling clouds,
All implying another life.

But enough!
Very well, enough
Decoration of the narrative.
Now, where were we?

Mischief
She and her brother
Were determined – and determined –
To be headstrong.

Philosophy
Sophie was alert
To the two meanings here
Of the word 'determined'.

Mischief Resumed
Even at hopscotch
She and Stanislaw were plotting
Apple-pie beds.

The Distant Future
Zofia would nurture three children
And occasional flights in verse
Into the symbolism of birds.

Early Indiscretions
In the convent
She stood on a pudding
To prove it inedible.

Consequent Flight
Running away, she ran
From the convent
Headlong into adolescence.

Time Lapses
A few moments had passed
And she was years
Deeper into caprice.

First Marriage
Aged twenty when her body
Was still surprised at itself,
She married Andrew Tarnowski.

Clouds Over Europe
As war approached
She burned her passport,
Vowing never to leave Poland.

Embers
But the burning passport
Failed to forestall
Forest fires in Poland.

Poland Abandoned
And soon, pincered by Germany
And Russia, she left by car
With four fateful companions.

They Were
Her husband, her brother,
Her brother's fiancée Chouquette,
Chouquette's sister.

Driving South
They hastened from Poland
And through Greece. In Jerusalem
Andrew confessed love for Chouquette.

Through Frosted Glass
From the car windows
Brooding forest
Gave way to palms.

Unlikely Friendships
Sophie and Chouquette
And Chouquette's son
Went on to Egypt.

Riches Beyond Dreams
An uncle of King Farouk
Offered them a luxury villa
With hot and cold running gold.

Cicadas
Cicadas loudlacing between trees
And entwining hospital visits
Tied Poland to Egypt.

Brief Return
Returning to Warsaw
She planted the sapling
Of the Red Cross in Poland.

The War
The most uproarious parties
Of the Second World War
Were Zofia's in Cairo.

Moving In
Her future husband,
Coldstream officer Billy Moss
Invited her to join them.

A Few Possessions
She entered their all-male household
With one swimsuit, one
Evening dress, two pet mongooses.

High Jinks
Soon they were playing
Pin the Tail On the Donkey
And making asses of themselves.

A Characteristic Precept
She embodied the precept
Why not? Her parties
Became ever more exuberant.

Distinguished Guests
Guests included King Farouk
Who once dropped in
With a crate of champagne.

Private Bin
'This is the champagne
Favoured by the Sphinx
At full moon.'

Favoured Vintage
'This is the champagne
Which I prefer
In the steam baths.'

Her Dedication
In the daylight between parties
She visited hospitals
And the families of prisoners.

Planning
Patrick Leigh Fermor
And Billy Moss drew maps
In dew on the bathroom tiles.

Room Service
A successful ambush
Was thus planned in steam
While Sophie served sarsaparilla.

Her Foresight
Well met by moonlight,
Sophie saw in its beams
The film of the book of the ambush.

Flashbulbs
At the glittering premiere
Zofia wore a blackbird's feather
Found in Rudnik, Poland.

Mediterranean
Patrick Leigh Fermor, expert
On Mediterranean echoes
Managed to sound out rare wines.

Temperatures Rising
At party after party
Coldstream Billy Moss
Began to generate heat.

Her Frugality
Economies were vital.
Sophie remembered Rudnik estate
And its plum liqueur press.

Improvisation
She suggested a scheme
For the manufacture of liqueur
From prunes soaked in the bath.

Disappointment
This would utilise raw alcohol
Obtained from the local garage.
The results were disappointing.

Triumph
She had more success
With an ersatz Polish pudding
Made almost entirely from dates.

Transformation
Once, swimming in the Nile,
She encountered a dolphin,
Or perhaps became one.

League of Nations
Once, English blackbirds
Sang the Marseillaise –
Détente in Cairo!

Nightride
One starbright night
She rode the Sphinx to Luxor –
Or was that a dream?

Glenn Miller Disappears
Until peace broke out
They danced to In The Mood
On a wind-up gramophone.

Peace In Our Time
The war left in its wake
Empty champagne crates.
Divorcing Andrew, she married Billy Moss.

Married Life
This glittering premiere
Lasted until the late 50s.
Soon afterwards Moss died at 44.

A Long Unfolding
And so began
A long life of fragments.
Zofia took in lodgers.

A Gale Through Europe
The fall of communism
Opened a gauze curtain
On Polish cobbles.

Rudnik Again
Sophie's nephew repurchased Rudnik.
At 82 she presided
At a family gathering.

Champagne Again
There was champagne
And Polish sweetmeats. The forest swayed
To an old gramophone.

The Old Order
But too much had changed
For her to remain,
And a long fraying ribbon,

Farewells
Untangled from the past
Tied her occasional verses
Into a fragrant album.

A Mandelbrot Set

Benoit B. Mandelbrot (1924–2010) was the inventor of fractals which are essentially self-replicating bits of geometry. He further made significant the question 'How long is the coastline of England?' Fractals have become omnipresent – in art, advertising, design and, although (with the exception of Leonardo) we hadn't noticed them, in the vortices of Nature itself.

Begin
The ant lion's claw is a cycloid
And magnified a million times
Is a city skyline's yardarm at dusk.

Continue
The ant lion's egg cup in the sand
Is an ellipsoid
Identical in shape to the impress of the elbow
Of one sleeping on the beach, and
To the hollow exposed by the tide.

A digression
In the children's joke
Ants cross the cereal box at a brisk stroke
And, reading 'Tear along dotted line'
One says, 'We're going as fast as we can.'

More of the same
Lying on the tousled beach
On a surf towel depicting seahorses
Someone's cheek has left the impress
Of an ant lion's crèche.

Euclid deposed
In the new geometry of the coastline
The shortest distance between points
Is via the ziggurat.

The shortest distance
Depends on the magnification of spectacles,
And one man's spectacles
May be another man's circus
With lions swerving like swallows.

From the helicopter
The magnificat of distance
Modulates endlessly.

In the pursuit of distance
Perambulation is the new point of rest.
The flâneur traces a straight line
Insofar as it is seen as the sum
Of segments angled variously like a logjam.

A flâneur from Riga,
Benoit B. Mandelbrot with playful rigour
Added the B himself although
It signifies no name. This recalls
His construction of equilateral triangles
On the central third of each side
Of an equilateral triangle
In a process which continues indefinitely.

The flâneur visits Limerick
When Benoit B. (B!) Mandelbrot
Was tacking at sea on a yacht
He made the decision
To try subdivision
As a cloud eddied out like a blot.

Some ground rules
'Clouds are not spheres,
Mountains are not cones,
Coastlines are not circles,
Bark is not smooth,
Nor does lightning travel
In straight lines.'

As a consequence
'Fractally Gaudi is superior
To Van der Rohe.'

And furthermore
'Being a language Mathematics
May be used not only to inform
But also to seduce.'

To exemplify which
Not far from the coastal reach
A seductive man undresses a peach
By the mere conjuration and spangle
Of Apollonius' Triangle
Advanced on a shingle.

And therefore what might have been:
Actaeon advances upon bathing Diana
Bearing hyperbole and hyperbola,
And finds himself home and hosed.

A personal credo formulated and instanced
'Omnipresent Similitude' or More of the Same:
Twins reunited after a few seconds' separation.

A corollary
'Accidents which form patterns'
i.e. the Past

A tribute
In 1990 the small asteroid
27500 Mandelbrot
Was named in his honour.
Seconds later another coalescing cloud
Appeared, virtually identical.

A piece of string
How long is a piece of coastline?

Increase
I
Was walking
Home one day
When leaving the usual
Pathway through the dark woods
I found myself increasingly meandering towards
The coastline intermittently shining through clustered trees.

But wait, there's more
Simple numerical increase can not
Hold a candle to the vast
Dark regions of space dominated
By that bristling hedgehog
Or earwig or stag beetle,
The Mandelbrot Set.

Simplicity in no way corresponds
To the vital concept
Of self-similarity.
And Benoit Mandelbrot walking (say)
Home one day
When leaving the usual
Bristle-cone path to press
Further into the cress
Of the woods, saw through a gulf
The self-similar sea shelf
And the wave breaking intermittently.

A literary example
Indeed, might it not be time
In the receding tail of the Mandelbrot comet
To propose alternative self-similitudes –
Let us say multiple plagiarisms of Borgès'
Pierre Menard, Author of Don Quixote.

In the forest
In a eucalypt library
(Read, a library in the forest)
Amidst the multiple aspersions of leaves
To chance on a later version
(Identical and yet unique)
Of the Quixote of Pierre Menard.

And so on
And to find in its appendices
An endless list of Menard's other works.

Essential reading
And in every corridor and every
Storage bay and every carrel
In this self-same library
To find what might be called
The DNA of literature.

Further instances of the above
Similarly for self-similarity
Let us turn to the anthology
Of early Renaissance Annunciations
And find in each the same elements:
An hourglass, the sprig of lily,
The hortus conclusus or enclosed garden,
Its rose hedge, cypress and umbrella pine,
And above the whole
The Presence of God in clouds.

Then consider, for example,
The Annunciation of Lorenzo Lotto,
Its early advocacy by Berenson
Its similarities and differences
(The cat for example
Startled by epiphanies)
From the Annunciations
Of the previous century.

Propitious day
Mandelbrot marries Aliette Kagan in '55;
The bride brings a trousseau of DNA.
Replication in the history of ideas
Beats at the window like a sun shower.

Aliette at the tiller
A multiplicity of images
All almost identical
Of a boat turning below cliffs
Its prow elevated as the motor accelerates,
Every image virtually identical
Until it suddenly turns out to sea.

She steps ashore. Benoit notes,
'Clouds are not spheres, mountains
Are not cones, coastlines are not circles'
As a swallow flies in from the coast
With a fanfare of cusps.

She steps ashore. And in a single step
Crosses the coastline and enters the forest.

In the lemon-scented forest
The library is closed for the recataloguing of leaves.
In the disorder on the river
The ripple spreads in cardioids
And nowhere is a circle to be seen
On the estuary's sifting sheen.

Heaps of haiku
Here we go again
With the fluttering of wings
To unfold the coast.

The shape of the coast
As I crawl about appears
Very like elsewhere.

The coastline near here
My magnifying glass makes
More like the coast there.

Here's a fleck of weed,
Here's a runnel of sandfall,
Here's a quartz funnel.

Here's a fragile bee
Intoxicated by seaspray
Trying to climb out.

Round the coastline map
May be seen interesting
Changes in ink strength.

Stains of printing inks
Along the length of the coast
Tintinnabulate.

The ink molecules
Vary like thunder and ring
Like a rack of bells.

But the coastal map
Is not the coast. The coast is
Pure adjacency.

Each beach is unique
But to the swimmer offshore
They are all alike.

Lie with me, O Arcs!
Along the curves of the coast
Let us find new bays.

Children's rhymes
To replicate with DNA
One needs to keep the past away
And let the coastline out to play
To come again another day.

Modest agenda
Who, were I to cry out
Would hear me amongst the myriad poets?
Yet I would still hope to differentiate
Between things repeated endlessly.

Leibniz 101
Identity is impossible
Since contenders are
Separated in space.

The added B
When Benoit B.B.(!) Mandelbrot
(The added B an aliquot
Designed to nudge him past the post
To be no more his namesake's ghost)

Had posited (without such fame)
The temporal coastline, with this claim
He thought events must replicate
Just as geometries relate.

For Time (he thought and hoped to prove)
Is everywhere at one remove
From our perception of it, and
Like coastlines, endlessly expands.

The B-loud glade
More buds than flowers at any time
The garden is flowering with anticipations.
The bees perform complex curves
And swallows add unique cusps.
Each iris bud coils and is a snail,
Each opening flower is a time lapse photograph.

Children's song
How long is the coastline of Britain?
It depends how the coastline is written.
How long is the coastline of Britain?
It resembles the play of a kitten.

> *You naughty kittens you've lost your mittens*
> *And you shall have no tea*
> Unless – hang on – what are these?
> In an unexplored coastal frieze –
> *5 mittens!*

Written on clouds a list of Contents
Fractal geometry. Check!
Fractals in Nature. Of course!
Fractal memory. Eh?

Swimming out to sea
Just offshore where the coastline
No longer follows its own contours
He swam like a porpoise
Echoing Poincaré's account of imaginary numbers,
'That amphibian between being and non-being.'

A concession
Of course so-called imaginary numbers
Which are simply two-dimensional numbers
Are essentials in the Mandelbrot story.

Bertolin B. Andemot's preferred approach
'I would name them complex numbers
Rather than imaginary since it is impossible
To imagine $\sqrt{-1}$.'

Two-dimensional numbers? Shock? Horror?
Well, no. It's just our old friend,
The number-plane. Which amounts to placing numbers
Somewhere on a street directory or road map.

Some readers may prefer
To skip over the following.
The Formation of the Set:
If z is a complex number
(Say on the Sydney Harbour Bridge
When the origin is the old GPO)
Then calculate $z=z^2+c$. Repeat.
(z may now move to, say, Taronga Park.)
Repeat. If the distance of each z
From the G.P.O. is, using Pythagoras,
Less than 2 then that point
Is a member of the Mandelbrot Set.
If not, not.

Now that wasn't too hard, was it?
And now as we range far and wide
And we encounter the plover hastening
In a straight line across our path
Or the driver in the car ahead
While stopped at lights handing back
A birdcage to the rear-seat passengers
Or a ball thrown almost into orbit
Its trajectory following a catenary
Rather than parabola – we ask
What of these? Can these be in the Set?

For patrons of the airwaves
Ladies and gentlemen of the Jura
In paying tribute to the man
Who put the coastline on the map
It would be remiss of me not to mention
Slarty Bartfast and his groundbreaking work
On the fjord-enjambed coast of Norway.

A twin living on the coast
Niobe T. Mandelbrot
Lived in a fabled inlet
Unseen by most passers-by
In a tiny house made of driftwood,
Moss flecks and shell and lichen
And carapace of crab
At a point where phase doubling offshore
Was wont to begin for no apparent reason.

A distant neighbour
Ben J. Handelbar
Had never heard of the Mandelbrot Set
And aspired to join the fast set
Or jet set, largely without success. He lived
In another inlet on the coast
On the obverse of the island
Unversed in physics and verse
But not averse to physic.
He was the inventor of novelty windsocks
Which he displayed on his particular foreshore
Noting with amusement that for every twenty
One would seem indifferent to the wind.

A kind aunt
During the uprising, Benoit's aunt, Bonnuit M.,
Had remained in Lithuania
And after remarrying (several times)
And dabbling and doubling in alchemy
Had telegraphed Benoit and begun
To send him flower-press specimens,
Photographs of the non-canonical mountains,
Sections of fern and leaf vein
Calcite memories of logarithmic spirals,
Leaves from fragrant albums.
This generosity increased and eventually
He began to receive petrified branches
And fossilised stones of such weight
That he considered building solarium extensions
To house these mementoes of his homeland.

Again or still?
Here is the plover hastening again,
Hastening, reluctant to fly unless drawn,
Crossing the empty lawn
Like some part of the past
Which has not quite successfully passed.

Accidents plus time equals form
M: 'One of the persons most baffled
By my work was myself.'
'My life seems a series of accidents,
Yet looking back I see a pattern.'

Fractals' self-similarity
The fractals' self-similarity
Should surely be amenable to alignment
Such as connects the arrow to its target
With the singlemindedness of DNA?
Yes, but where, O where, might be found
The means? I mean, Geometry needs
More than a wide beach with Roman soldiers.

More, there's weight
A plover crossing the field
Then enters the adjoining field.
A driver passing a birdcage
Over the seat to rear passengers
Just as the lights change
Belatedly signals to turn.
The coastline is magnified until
A pristine beach swims into view
One on which no Crusoe has set foot.

Here I must declare
'A mountain is not a cone
And here I must declare
My opposition to Cezanne
And the Cubists. Simplification

Is the bane beyond the pale.
Let us defy even Plato
And count every ciliary hair
While hearing the thrush in the thicket
Rather than posit the Forms.'

The Sierpinski Triangle
Delman Ben-Trobiot
Steps up to the microphone.
'My friend's name does indeed
Mean in English almond bread;
And were he to raise dogs
Of every size from the Great Dane
To the miniature Chihuahua
He would no doubt devise
A series of self-similar kennels
Based on the Sierpinski Triangle (q.v.).'

Incident in infancy
In Lithuania my grandmother
Grew peonies and irises.
The peonies opened like miraculous
Tissue flowers in water.
The irises grew up through them like spears.
One day I rode my tricycle
Into every inlet following the garden wall
And severed several irises;
She ran out from the house
And put the several stems in water,
The buds still tight, not showing colour.
Three weeks passed. Accretions of events
Bypassed the vase and then
The leading buds showed colour
And for a week the furled and unfurled
Tricoloured silk sacks opened fully
And, at their window in their vase
I was allowed daily to freshen the water.

Short lyric
Volutes and involutes of opening irises:
Self-similarity in bright disguises.

Unparalleled Iris descends to the plain
When the rainbow is magnified repeatedly
Eventually it becomes a ziggurat down whose steps
In leaps and bounds Iris descends at dusk
Her task to tease out gold cords,
Their braids eased to release the traveller
Far and wide to adjacent fields.

Baltic forests
In Lithuania chestnut glades
Cut from the forest, overlapping,
Formed in space a Venn Diagram –
A metaphor of course – with cress, moss
Blackbirds in forest gloom,
Hollyhocks buffeting through grass –
For what would become
In forty years of exiled mapping
The Mandelbrot Set.

The blackbirds' singing seemed to declare
Them outside all possible metaphor
The forest floor was far
From any coast. The sun appeared
Far out to sea. Then and there
Points in the number plane were assumed
Either in or out, far or near
Posited in memory or positively fugitive
For this maverick destined for IBM.

An aurora in the adjoining field
As we walk towards the sea
Reverie balloons out on either side
Towards the horizon. A tendency too
To self-replication produces clouds,
Shadows like speech balloons.
Soon we have excess, a press,
A summer dress with pattern repeats,
Thoughts so prolix, so
Overlappingly alike, that we seem
To teem in gloaming and walk in many worlds.

Homage to Chekhov

Afternoon Tea Shared With Joseph Brodsky

Sunset clings to the samovar, abandoning the veranda,
– see the shadows slink away like a shy lawn leveret.
But the tea has gone cold, or is finished; a fly scales a saucer's dolce
while the saucer rattles like a Tarkovskyan tribute to Russia.
And her heavy chignon makes Varvara Andreevna look grander
– take a gander – yes grander
than ever! Her starched cotton blouse is staunchly
– its snow hillocks enclosed raunchily –
buttoned up to her chin. Vialtzev, deep in his chair, is nodding
with a little cottage-in-the-valley cigar smoke pencil
over the rustling weekly with Dubrovo's latest swing
at the cabinet. Varvara Andreevna under her skirt wears not a
thing, like a tree in spring.

The drawing room's dark piano responds to a dry ovation
of hawthorns. The student Maximov's few random chords
tell a story worth a thousand pictures and a million words
and in their laconic cool elation
stir the garden's cicadas. In the platinum sky, athwart,
squadrons of ducks, foreshadowing aviation,
almost as if they are signalling readiness
to be in any of the major plays,
drift towards Germany. Hiding in the unlit
library, Dunia devours Nikki's letter, so full of cavils.
She's a land canal with locks at so many levels.
No looker; but, boy, what anatomy! And so unlike
hardcovers. Might they be lovers?

That is why Erlich winces, called in by Kartashov –
Oh, that waistcoat and chain! And Oh, the French window
offering such suggestive light beyond the baize table –
to join Prigozhin, the doctor, and him at cards. 'With pleasure.'
He cuts the deck. He deals.
*Ah, but swatting a fly is simpler than staving off
a reverie of your niece, naked upon the leather
couch and fighting mosquitoes, fighting heat – but to no avail.*
– Even inverted over your head cold water in a pail
would be off a duck's back! No deal!
*Prigozhin deals as he eats: with his belly virtually
crushing the flimsy table. Can the doctor be asked about this
    little boil?*
Perhaps eventually. Perhaps after this reverie.

Oppressive midsummer twilight; a truly myopic past
– almost amounting to macular degeneration
with whole sections of the picture missing –
*of day, when each shape and form loses resolve, gets eerily
vague. 'In your linen suit, Piotr Lvovich, it's not so hard
to take you for one of the statues down in the alley.' 'Really?'*
'Oh yes! the ones frequented by ravens.'
*Erlich feigns embarrassment, rubbing his pince-nez's rim.
It's true, though: the far-off in twilight looks near, the near, alien;*
it's coloratura weather and the air is thin
*and Erlich tries to recall how often he had Natalie
Fiodorovna in his dream* – like ices topped with cream.

*But does Varvara Andreevna love the doctor? Gnarled poplars crowd
the dacha's wide-open windows with peasant-like abandon.*
There's a movement of the seasons and their leaves
are threatened with a rush and rustle of dry stems.
*They are the ones to be asked: their branches, their crow-filled crowns.
Particularly the elm climbing into Varvara's bedroom:*
it alone sways back from the window,
it alone sees the hostess with just her stockings on.
Then dusk arrives like a windgust of ash,
like stencils over a lake still luminous,
*Outside, Dunia calls for a swim in the night lake: 'Come, lazies!'
To leap, overturning the tables! Hard, though, if you are the one
with aces* or trying to hear a blackbird's last traces.

And the cicada chorus, with the strength of the stars' display,
like a miniature aural spiral arm
burgeons over the garden, sounding like their utterance;
and we've all gone swimming in summer – in a kind of trance.
*Which is, perhaps, the case. Where am I, anyway?
wonders Erlich, undoing his braces at the outhouse entrance.*
A lighted coach seems to imply a different distant road.
*It's twenty versts to the railroad. A rooster attempts its lied.
The student Maximor's pet word, interestingly, is 'fallacy'*
and he muses humorously about spelling it 'phallacy'.
*In the provinces too nobody's getting laid
as throughout the galaxy* or in every sentence beginning 'She…

Lingering Still with Brodsky over the Samovar

1   Bees make a beeline
    Combining cycloid and cardioid and limaçon
    With other curves notable for their cusps
    All divided and joined in segments
    And complicated by oscillations and lisps
    And hummingbird pauses;

    Cicadas make a line of noise
    Similarly favouring discursion and meander
    In maze paths through their day
    With enthusiasm along the way
    For hot sunny breezeless days.
    Bellbirds get through the day by punctuation

    Punctuating it excessively
    So that no sentence shape
    Is allowed to escape
    Comma semicolon dash and stop
    For more than a brief glitter
    Of duration; their paths overlap
    Those of trees complicit and insisting

    That their variety be explicit
    In suggesting sequences leading off
    A thousand ways, their tousled canopies
    Implying continuous entanglement, their day paths
    Crisscrossing from dawn till dusk;

Even flowers look one in the face bravely
With their faces gravely hoping to trace
The sun through and behind trees
Expressing the hope that their singularities
Will be overlooked in favour of their variety
Tracing trajectories through the day.

And this is to say nothing
Of autumn-coloured trees in midsummer,
Of evergreen trees in autumn
Of roses so prolific that their late summer flowering
Is indistinguishable from their early spring,
Or the white parasol at the end

Of a corridor of trees almost transparent
Wavering or waving in the noon sun,
Representing in this context the legion
Of single objects and singular quiddities
Each rowing calmly with plash light
Over the endless ratchets of the day.

All of these traces in the day's cloud chamber,
These loom threads admitting the day's wefts
Might be taken as emblems for the remarkable clefts,
Departures, effusions, glancing rays, blows, discussions,
Collisions, skyrockets and tangents of the poems
By the author of *So Forth* and so forth.

2 Beside the beach where one house has been demolished
    And another not yet built there's a sort of suggestion
    Of a lens enlarging the view. The builder's name

    On a notice is Les Moore suggesting the odd
    Foolishness of someone greeting him at a party
    Or confetti wedding with the phrase *Les is Moore*.

3 Like late Auden without the carpet slippers
    Or mature Stevens without the complacencies

    (His word, you'll concede) the author of *So Forth*
    Is a sputtering splendid Catherine Wheel

    (Which only occasionally falls to the wet lawn
    And even then continues to fire unexpectedly)

    Seeming to go on and on, as easy-going,
    Genial and sunny as a waterfall.

4 It was because I tomahawked the tea tomatoes
    And shredded the lettuce and diced the potatoes
    (Then had second thoughts and retrieved them)

    That the first salad of lines in praise of him
    Was never written down, will never now ever
    Be written down, a loss which gives these lines

    Being written across instead a peculiar transparency
    Like tomato cut very thin or cucumber placed
    Cosmetically on closed eyes through which thoughts

X-ray conjuring auroras. In fact the facts
Suggest the oddity of many alternative axes
For events in time, multiple lives he juggled

All impinging somehow but as transparent
(Yes) as a dragonfly wing, the very sort of
Delightful multivalence which he thought of.

5 And you who re-alerted me to the pleasures
Of the author's *To Urania* akin to the pleasures

Of the taste buds being given a grand tour
Of lemon and vanilla and cinnamon and rosewater

And glistening bouquets of sweets as delicious
As aubergine and the word 'aubergine',

May I present you with my variations
On the line, 'Having bumped into memory

Time learns its impotence.' Well, may I?
I need your 110% agreement. I may?

'Having' (here goes) 'learned of memory, time
Becomes strangely impotent and bumps into things.'

6 In the *TLS*, advocates vied
With detractors, the latter
Claiming him wayward,
His grasp of English like batter
Floating off from the fish
It is meant to coat in the dish.

You in whom understanding
Walks hand in hand with delight
On poetry's spray-splashed landing
Know the advocates are right.
Confronted by Brownian motion
One rightly invokes the ocean

And applauds the very notion
Of constant flux, that pale
Beyond whose careering station
Sheaves of tangents sail
Impelled by a solar flare
Chosen because it is there.

7   Up three thousand feet from the Adriatic
Oak trees in a light wind
Are crowding in for some grand finale;

Imagine our startlement and theirs
When all that appears in their arena
Are pigs intent on trundling past

In a hurry from one glade to another,
Last remnants of Odysseus' changed men
Still intent to get back to their wives.

8   His detractors err in lore
Mistaking generosity for display
Projecting their own desire for admiration
On the plasma screen of his profusion;

Delight is his métier
Diffusing metre, and, not knowing delight,
They misread the spinning Catherine Wheel
For a stationary target.

9   Discursion raises eventually, if discursively,
The default position that there is no
Centre from which discursion takes meaning;

The blithe discursivist at length and by
Persistent flourishing of multiple packs of cards
From which one takes any card again and again

Convinces the most determined centralist, thematicist,
Absolutist or determinist that in sheer proliferation
And profusion lies abundant delight. Thus

Surrealism is discursion's love-child, but over and above
Its subversion of the bourgeois reigns the spectacle
Of sunbursts and solar flares and the rain

Of particle showers, tantamount to the assertion
That everything and anything by virtue of being thought
Is equally splendid, alluring and charmingly viable.

10 Repeatedly going out on the end
Of a limb or in at the deep end
Or off at a tangent he (the poet,

Brodsky, the subject of all these paeans)
Is expressing (in the particle cloud chamber
Of his scattering observations)

Concern, generosity, affection for the reader
As persistent as the koel's repeated
Upwards glissando *You all right?*

11 While towing Lion Island out to sea
    The Hawkesbury Dreamer hit a hidden reef
    And slack snaked down the hawsers. Smilingly
    The captain from the foc's'le cried, 'Good grief!'
    Then laughed as Lion Island followed through.

    The sea was mazed with many a lazing yacht.
    The captain came on deck to greet the crew
    And said, 'I'll level with you. Look to port – '
    (The sea was like a spirit level too)
    'You see that island bearing down on us

    While we are floundering here in medias res?
    Well! Rest assured, it's just a metaphor,
    Though a convincing one like all of space.
    I'm just as much a fiction as you are
    So let's enjoy, as if it were the Past,

    The brimming Present, till the next neap tide
    Floats us offshore. Meanwhile I urge you all
    To note there's nothing fixed (our keel aside);
    Go with the flow and all that's variable,
    And take delight in multiplicity.'

12 I was walking under the overcliff
    Eager to broach the shale beach
    Looking for whales and squalls at sea
    And shadows out of reach

I was seeking frail contingencies
Events like tangents from the sea
Time like a sine wave on its way
Unfolding endlessly

When out to sea the sea appeared
As if it rolled beneath a weight
Which grooved the plain and stifled waves
And that weight were delight.

13 A sea mist weighed upon the sea
As if an arm with spreading sleeve
Leaned down and scattered every harvest wave

With just the weight a man might feel
When asked too many times, and fail
And bridle at the last 'Astonish me!'

14 *For the fourth day the sea hits the dike with its hard horizon*
[So Forth]

For the fourth day the sea hits, with its hard horizon the dike;
That is to say the sea, levering up the horizon
Attached to it by tremendous meniscal forces, flourishes it
Above its head and with biblical éclat smites the dike.

Or for the fourth day the dike with its hard horizon
Is hit by the sea. That is to say the dike,
Imposing as it does a metre rule length on the soft doona
Of the horizon at large, provides an easy target
For the sea which, lunging from itself, inflicts a blow.

On the fifth day the sea, lunging from itself everywhere,
Like a midsummer meadow of tigersnakes leaping for moths,
Signals a change of intention and moves sideways away
From the dike gathering force without inflicting the least injury.

That is to say the dike, springing at the one moment
A thousand holes, releases on probation the sea
Which chastened slides away without raising a single sword
And then at some distance from the imprisoning rail looks about
And, turning this way and that, questions how to begin again.

www.ingramcontent.com/pod-product-compliance
Lightning Source LLC
Chambersburg PA
CBHW070051120526
44589CB00034B/1936